D1277861

Dear Brooklyn,
Love Yourself

Be Bold. Be Beautiful. Be You.

Dear Brooklyn, Love Yourself

Be Bold. Be Beautiful. Be You.

Shandia Booker

Published by Truth2RenewHearts Publishing
An imprint of Truth2RenewHearts Enterprises, LLC
Pittsburgh, Pennsylvania

For information:
Info@truth2renewheartspublishing.com

ISBN-13: 978-0-9864482-4-9
ISBN-10: 0-9864482-4-9

The examples used in this book are compilations of stories from real situations. But names, facts, and issues have been altered to protect confidentiality while illustrating the points. The ideas, suggestions, general principles and conclusions presented here reflect the view of the author and your implementation of the information provided should be adapted to fit your own particular situation or circumstance. The author has made every effort to ensure the accuracy of the information herein. However, the information contained in this book is provided without warranty, either express or implied.

Publisher's Note: The views expressed in this work are solely those of the author and do not necessarily reflect the views of the publisher. The publisher is not responsible for websites (or their content) that are not owned by the publisher.

Cover design by Robin Miller

Unless otherwise indicated, Scripture quotations are from:
The Holy Bible, King James Version

This book belongs to:

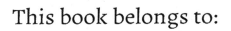

Dedication

My Lord and Savior Jesus Christ-
The love that you show me is unmatched, there's none like you. Thank you for
choosing to love me the way only You can

My Mom, Annette Parker-
Thank you for being you. I'm grateful for your love, encouragement, support
and strength

Women working with & raising inner city teen girls-
Thank you for your commitment to the next generation of Queens. I pray that
you are able to see what they become!

Inner City Teen Girls-
The strength, style, and heart that you possess is AMAZING. Don't you ever
forget it! May this book serve as a reflection of God's love for you

Contents

Foreword

On a hot Saturday in August 2010, I walked into a classroom at Duquesne University to begin the *Multicultural Issues and Strategies in Counseling* course in pursuance of my Master's degree in Clinical Mental Health Counseling. Like many others, I scanned the room to find a seat, and I chose the one positioned right behind an old high school classmate and in front of two African American women. Moments later, I heard a perky voice from behind me enthusiastically say, "Hi, my name is Shandia! I think you and I have a mutual friend in common!" As I turned around, I was greeted with the warmest smile, and in that moment (although I never told her) I knew she and I would become friends! Within the last eight years, Ms. Booker and I have experienced many triumphs, and we've endured trying times together. So, when my sister friend asked me to write the foreword to her first book (yes, I'm speaking future publications into existence), I was honored and ecstatic because this brainchild has been years in the making!

I first heard about "Dear Brooklyn, Love Yourself" while it was still a concept Ms. Booker was contemplating and praying about. Ms. Booker's journey as a young black girl from the inner city of Pittsburgh, Pa, has equipped her with a unique perspective, and she has used her wisdom, insight, and words of encouragement to construct this interactive book. As I read this book, I heard the gentle, yet steady voice of a mentor or family member (e.g., auntie, big sister) reminding me that God's Word is still applicable today. Having navigated many of the topics that are unpacked within this book, Ms. Booker provides a refreshing, honest, and transparent perspective about her own journey and the ways in which she's utilized her relationship with Christ to traverse some of life's challenges. Although written with adolescent girls in mind, this book is a practical guide not only for youth, but it can be used as conversation starters for parents, or as an inspiration guidebook for ladies on the "glo up", who recognize the importance of letting their light shine.

For these reasons, I encourage you to begin this book with an open heart and mind, prepared to engage in honest self-reflection. Keep in mind, growth requires some level of discomfort; but trust that through Ms. Booker's words, you will be able to uncover and appreciate your authentic self without compromising your moral compass. This book reminds me of the relationship I've developed with Ms. Booker over the years, encapsulated within this scripture my sister friend (Ms. Booker) and I often recite: "As iron sharpens iron, so one person sharpens another" (Proverbs 27:17 NIV). Reading through this book has sharpened and convicted me. My hope and prayer is that you allow for this book to do the same for you.

With Love,
Michelle D. Mitchell, PhD, LPC-PA, NCC

Introduction

Girl, I'm so excited this book has reached your hands. It is my prayer that this book will have a positive impact on your life. I wrote this book to encourage you to embrace who you are and to love yourself. There are many mixed messages being conveyed through the media about who inner-city brown girls are, and I am challenging you to be confident in who you've been created to be. As you read, you will find life lessons throughout each chapter, and I wrote the chapters to you in the form of a letter. I encourage you to take time out of your day to read each one, and make sure you pace yourself. After each letter, you will find a set of reflection questions, along with space for you to write your thoughts. When responding to the reflection questions in each chapter, be honest, have fun, and try not to be too hard on yourself.

This book is designed to help you embrace your uniqueness and to help you grow. I want you to be empowered and I want you to know that you have great purpose. The message "Love yourself" is woven throughout the pages of this book, and I also share words of encouragement and scripture verses to help you move forward in God's purpose for your life. As you've noticed, the title of this book is *Dear Brooklyn*. Though this may not be your formal name, and you may live in another city, consider *Brooklyn* as a term of endearment from me to you. In addition to loving the name, Brooklyn is one of the most populated boroughs in New York, it's a place where beautiful souls reside, and I believe this name embodies you and me. Know that this book was pre-destined and written specifically for you. As you journey through this book, I want you to remember that you are ENOUGH and you are valuable. I'm encouraging you to let the love of God lead you throughout your life. This book is a great place to start. Let the journey begin!

I Woke Up Like This, Flawless

"You alone are enough, you have nothing to prove to anyone"
- **Maya Angelou**

Dear Brooklyn,

You may have heard Beyoncé or your classmates say, "I woke up like this, I woke up like this.... we Flawless ladies tell them!" The hook is so catchy, because it goes against the norms of us being flawless *after* we are all put together. Bey sends a message to the masses that says *I woke up, and I am beautiful, prior to putting on my stylish outfit, accessories, and make up!* Listen, I love and appreciate a stylish outfit, accessories, and make up, but they don't define our beauty, they accent it. When we wake up, we are who we are and this means you are God's masterpiece.

Now, I want you to *really* consider what it means to be His masterpiece and to be created in the image of a King.

Our Father is love, He is gentle, and His works are marvelous. Girl, M-A-R-V-E-L-O-U-S, and that's how He created you! According to Merriam Webster, marvelous can be defined as: *the highest kind or quality.* Girl, you were made in the image of the King, so remember that you are of the highest kind and quality. The truth is, when our Father formed you, He created you exactly how He wanted you to be. You are so special that He formed you before you were in your mother's womb. He saw fit that you should be born, and He knew exactly when and where you would be born. He even divinely placed you in your specific generation because He knew before you entered the world how He wants to use you to impact the world.

You are beyond beautiful, and by accepting yourself, and loving yourself, your beauty will shine through. Our King thought about you down to the detail of your complexion when He created you. Our Father, God, thought about the texture of your hair, your height, your smile and even your voice. He is a loving and intentional Father and He is in the details of your makeup. That freckle you have, was given by the King! The laugh you have, girl He gave you that too! You may have wondered about what made God give you the things that He has. Girl, let's talk about it! Let's have a *M.O.T (Moment of Transparency).* When I was your age, I wondered why He gave me some of the things He did. For example, my hair was thick and my mom wasn't the best stylist. I wanted my ponytails to be less "puffy" and I wanted them to look as sleek as some of my classmates'. I would try to figure it out by adding a little more grease or different hair products. Despite my efforts, I wasn't able to achieve the outcome that I wanted, so I had to learn to work with the texture of my hair. I always enjoyed getting my hair braided and my mom was willing to have someone else braid my hair (Shout out to Ms. Carol)! She kept my braids, beads, and foil looking fly (yes foil, ask your mom about the foil, LOL)!

As I grew older, I was able to go to the salon and request hair styles that I wanted and this was great. Eventually I noticed a pattern, I would find a solution in one area but find a flaw in another. There were things that I absolutely loved about myself but there were other things that I really struggled with. For example, I went to college having confidence in my abilities. There came a point when I questioned my voice. Did my voice sound like a black college girl's voice should (whatever that means)? Would my opinions be valued amongst my peers, (many of which who didn't look like me and some who did)? At that time, I concerned myself with the opinions of those who were not invested in me. Let me pause here for this W.O.W (Word of Wisdom). Listen, don't spend your life so focused on the opinions of others that you allow that to distract you from being the wonderful person God created you to be. I had to accept the fact that God gave me my voice and He knew that my voice did not need to sound like others'.

Society has ideas about what you should look like, sound like, and be like in order to be deemed beautiful and successful. As a child of the King, you have to remember that He created you just how He needed you to be. He didn't create us to just blend in, He created us to stand out. Every human being has flaws, but one of the best things about having a relationship with Christ is He truly gets us, because He created us! God works all things together for our good! As a result, He still chooses us despite our flaws. When you accept God's love for you, He will help you to love and accept yourself. Once you do this, your confidence will radiate!

Sometimes, our human nature urges us to put contingencies on the way we love ourselves. An example of a contingency is saying, "I will love myself fully when I get myself together" when the reality is, no one has it "altogether" and as you "glo up" you will evolve. I encourage you to love yourself through the process, not just after you have achieved your desired results! Girl this is a W.O.W (Word of Wisdom): don't deny yourself the love you deserve. Denying yourself love will not produce the results that you desire. Withholding self-love is unkind and it interferes with your ability to move forward towards your goals. It is important to have goals and to reflect on ways in which you can improve in different areas of your life. Later in the book, you will have the opportunity to create a plan that should help you start the process. The foundation of the process is accepting the love our Father gives you and choosing to love yourself like never before. Remember, our Father is loving and gentle; He will meet you where you are at in this very moment. He can grow things in us or grow things out of us. We all are a work in progress. Just as a plant can't grow without light, food, and water, we need His light and love to grow. If we held back our love from a plant it would cease to grow. Give yourself the love you need and look to our Father to be your example on how to do that. Remember that even with our flaws, God still chooses us and works all things together for our good! He is so amazing! Set your mind on Him so that you can embrace the truth about who you are. Girl, you are a good investment because you are God's investment. Out of His heart, His mouth spoke and a princess was born. There's nothing like a God investment, so go on with your flawless self!

Written Specifically for You,
Ms. Shandia Booker

Scriptures to Explore

You're beautiful from head to toe, my dear love, beautiful beyond compare, absolutely flawless. -Song of Solomon 4:7 (MSG)

Thank you for making me so wonderfully complex! Your workmanship is marvelous—how well I know it. -Psalm 19:14 (NLT)

Finally, brothers and sisters, whatever is true, whatever is noble, whatever is right, whatever is pure, whatever is lovely, whatever is admirable—if anything is excellent or praiseworthy - think about such things. -Philippians 4:8 (NLT)

Questions

What attributes or characteristics do you consider to be flaws?

_____

_____

_____

_____

_____

_____

Can you identify a time when you loved yourself past your flaws? If so, share below.

_____

_____

_____

_____

_____

How can you embrace who you are and trust that God will work all things together for your good?

_____

_____

_____

_____

_____

Words of Encouragement

Girl, our Father does not make mistakes. When He created you, you were not an afterthought. He took His time, thought about what He wanted, and He shaped you in His image. For those reasons, it is important that you don't try to convince others of your value. There's no need to prove to anyone what God has already established to be true. Often times, the things that we have a difficult time accepting about ourselves are typically what helps connect us to others. There may be some things that you don't fully understand about yourself now, but He will help you to understand later. I encourage you to begin looking through the lens that God uses when you look at yourself. When you are not seeing yourself clearly, re-adjust your lens. Once you adjust your lens, capture the moment. #Iwokeuplikethis #2020vision #ThroughGodsEyes

Chapter 2

What About Your Friends?

"Do not bring people in your life who weigh you down. And trust your instincts...good relationships feel good. They feel right. They don't hurt. They're not painful. That's not just with somebody you want to marry, but it's with the friends you choose. It's with the people you surround yourself with."

– Michelle Obama

Dear Brooklyn,

Friendship is one of God's greatest gifts! There is nothing like spending time with your girls, being yourself, enjoying life, laughing out loud, sharing, growing, and moving closer to His purpose for your life. Healthy friendships promote growth and provide us a safe place to discuss our grows ("grows" can be considered challenges that you face) and glos (your "glos" are your wins that allow you to shine)! The Bible tells us that as iron sharpens iron, friends sharpen friends. Good Friends (also known as SisterFriends) sharpen each other naturally. God allows us to add value to others, and have value added to our journey. Despite media messages that continue to show women having difficulty respecting, uplifting, and empowering each other, it is possible for girls to cultivate rich friendships with one another!

The foundation of being a good friend is found in the ability to have a good relationship with God and with yourself. Think about it. Have you ever been overly critical with yourself and found yourself being overly critical with your friend? Girl, try to be gentle, patient, loving, and kind with yourself so that you can show those characteristics to others, and especially toward your friends. Celebrate your friends 'glos'! If your friend works hard and earns a good grade on a project, celebrate that! If your friend sets a goal and achieves it, celebrate that! It is important that you show your friend that you support their endeavors.

In your friendships, it's also important to speak the truth in love. Times will come when you will have to talk to your friends about a difficult matter. I encourage you to be as gentle and loving as you can during those time. For example, if your friend is failing English class and you have noticed that she isn't completing assignments and turning in homework, you may want to have a caring conversation with her. Ask your friend if she is okay, and then bring up that you notice she's struggling in English. Try to be kind with your words instead of tearing her down. You may even invite her to the library with you once a week to help her get back on track. On the other hand, your friend may want to discuss a challenging matter with *you*, encourage you to get back on track, or say girl that's not the right look for you. I trust my **friends** to provide that for me; we have cultivated friendships where we can discuss real matters. We trust that we are coming from a loving place. Your friendships should provide a space for you to be open, honest, and have fun.

There may also be times when, despite your best intentions, you and your friends may face challenges. During those times it is important that you communicate with each other and listen to one another's concerns. The Bible teaches us in Mathew, Chapter 18 (NLT) verses 15-16, "If another believer sins against you, go privately and point out the offense. If the other person listens and confesses it, you have won that person back. But if you are unsuccessful, take one or two others with you and go back again, so that everything you say may be confirmed by two or three witnesses." The Bible provides a framework that teaches us how to solve conflict. In matters concerning your friendship, this is very important because it's likely that your friends are as close to you as family. By talking through issues, you can hear your friends' perspective and share your perspective to solve the conflict. During instances that your Sister friends unintentionally hurt your feelings, remember Proverbs 27:6 (NLT), "Wounds from a sincere friend are better than many kisses from an enemy". Remember that you want to lead with love, and that friends truly are a gift from God!

Over time, you may have a friendship that you outgrow for many reasons. Sometimes friendships come to an unexpected (or expected) end. If you tried to talk to your friend and you notice that their actions and response is consistently rude and hurtful, you may need to set a boundary and end the friendship. If you need help determining if a friendship needs to end, I would suggest talking to a trusted adult such as a Parent, Counselor, or Sunday School teacher about the situation. Chances are, that an adult can help you to resolve your conflict and help you see things from multiple perspectives. If the friendship is toxic they may advise you to let it go. In instances where a friendship has to come to an end, try your best to exit the friendship gracefully. You can walk away from someone or something without being rude or talking badly about the person and without gossiping and telling everyone else their business. You can lovingly walk away.

Girl, there will also be people who will come in your life that you will consider an acquaintance. According to Merriam-Webster, an acquaintance can be defined as a person whom one knows but who is not a particularly close friend. An acquaintance may be someone who is familiar and knows you slightly. Typically, you wouldn't invest the same time and energy in an acquaintance that you would invest in a friendship. It's likely that they won't invest the same time and energy in you either. Girl, don't take that personal; we all have limited time, energy, and resources. You will develop various relationships throughout life in which you may identify as an acquaintance. Those relationship can be wonderful as well, they just may not be as deep as your friendships.

On the other hand, you may have heard someone refer to a person as their *"frenemy"*. According to Merriam-Webster, a *frenemy is one who pretends to be a friend but is actually an enemy.* If you are trying to decipher between a friendship concern and someone being considered an enemy, I strongly encourage you to seek the advice of a trusted adult. It is my hope that you don't encounter many people you would consider to be a "frenemy". However, if your intuition tells you that someone is posing as your friend, but is really an enemy, pray and ask for clarity. Then, set boundaries and create necessary space in the relationship. Boundaries are important because they help to communicate how you want to move forward in a relationship and what you will and won't accept. An example, of a boundary you may want to set is choosing not to engage in conversation with someone who is toxic. Don't feel pressured to continue to engage in a *"friendship"* that is toxic, in which the person plans to intentionally bring you harm or one who finds solace in your downfall. Girl, you can still be respectful, **loving, and caring from afar by praying for your enemy.**

Refer to Luke 6:27 (NLT), this scripture encourages us to love our enemies and to do good to those who hate us! Girl, I know it seems like a huge task to do good to those who hate us, but God will give you the strength to begin the process. Send blessings that person's way and move forward with friends that help you "glo up". Our Father encourages us to be strong and courageous and he will provide you with the strength through your journey. Your true friends are not your enemy. Remember, in your friendships, you may experience conflict from time to time and that is to be expected.

Girl, pray and ask God to give you good friends. Your friends can bring so much joy to your life and you can bring joy to their lives as well. Friends that God sends your way will definitely become like sisters, and as you grow, your friendship will grow too! If you have a good BFF in your life, give her a call and thank her for being your friend!

Written specifically for you,
Ms. Shandia Booker

Scriptures to Explore

A friend is always loyal, and a brother is born to help in time of need. -Proverbs 17:17 (NLT)

There are "friends" who destroy each other, but a real friend sticks closer than a brother. -Proverbs 18:24 (NLT)

The heartfelt counsel of a friend is as sweet as perfume and incense. -Proverbs 27:9 (NLT)

As iron sharpens iron, so a friend sharpens a friend. -Proverbs 27:17 (NLT)

A troublemaker plants seeds of strife; gossip separates the best of friends. -Proverbs 16:28 (NLT)

Questions

Do you tend to make good choices or negative choices when you are around your friends? Explain why or why not.

_____

_____

_____

_____

_____

_____

In what ways do you support your friends?

_____

_____

_____

_____

_____

What characteristics do your closest friends display?

_____

_____

_____

_____

_____

_____

_____

How do you resolve conflict that may occur in your friendships?

_____

_____

_____

_____

_____

_____

What are some ways you can celebrate the healthy friendships that you have in your life?

_____

_____

_____

_____

_____

_____

Do you think it is possible to outgrow friends? How do you handle the "ending" of a friendship?

_____

_____

_____

_____

_____

_____

_____

_____

Words of Encouragement

Girl, having friends is one of life's greatest joys! My friends have become my sisters. When you begin to form healthy friendships, you will see growth in yourself and in your friends. You will notice an increase in joy, love, support, and fun! Good friends are loyal, give good advice, and help to push you closer to God's purpose for your life. If you are having trouble finding good friends, take a moment to pray and ask God to give people that you can connect to in order to experience healthy friendships. Begin to show yourself friendly, and watch God bless you! #Squadgoalsonthegloup #Whataboutyourfriends #Sisterfriends #Ingoodcompany #BFF

Chapter 3

He Loves Me, My King of All Kings

"Oh, how he loves us so, He loves us, He loves like a hurricane,
I am tree"
- David Crowder

Dear Brooklyn,

Girl, can you imagine what it's like to be loved by a king? Not just, any king, the greatest king of all? The King of all kings? The one who knows us down to the number of hairs on our head, the one who knows our challenges and our strengths? Embrace the fact that your Father is a King, and that you are His princess. You were born into royalty; therefore, you are royalty. God, our Father loves you, the King of all kings loves you in a way that no one else can. He is our provider, protector, way maker, and peace giver. Our Father shows His love to us on a personal level through our personal relationship that He has with us. Our Father desires to have a personal relationship with us, in which we learn to trust and depend on Him. He promises to prosper us and to not to bring us any harm.

I struggled to accept that our Father, God, the King of Kings, could love me the way He describes in his Word. God loves us just as we are! Let's have another *M.O.T (Moment of Transparency)* and you may begin to understand why this was a struggle for me. While growing up, my biological father was absent from my life. At a young age, I didn't think much of it because it was my norm, and the norm for many of the other people I knew. I have a stepfather, but at that time, I still felt abandoned by my biological father. As I started to get older, I noticed the impact it had on me. There wasn't any consistency in terms of contact with him. He did not call me or visit me regularly. When he came to visit my brother and me, it was usually unexpected, unless it was for a graduation ceremony. My dad made our graduations a priority, but I did not feel like I was a priority in his life on a regular basis.

At the time, because he didn't play a present role in my life, I didn't feel like he was a person that I could reach out to for protection, love, or advice. I began to wonder why he didn't play an active role in my life, especially since he grew up with his father. Eventually, I was able to talk my dad about how I felt, and this opened the door to slowly begin the process of moving forward. Girl, we're still in the process, but I've learned that God loves me and desires for me to forgive him. God has never abandoned me, He has always provided for me, and most importantly, He serves as my model of what love is. I am grateful for His love.

He loves you in the same way! As I mentioned earlier in this letter, God desires to have a personal relationship with you. He wants you to talk to Him, and He will listen. He also wants to talk to you and for you to listen. If you feel a sense of abandonment due to someone being absent in your life, I hope that you begin to pray and ask God to comfort you. Girl, please keep this W.O.W (word of wisdom) in mind: God's love for you is not based on the way other people love you. Accept that you are loved by the King of Kings and that He wants the best for you!

Abandonment may not be the challenge that you are dealing with. Maybe you're struggling with low self-esteem, worthiness, value, or another issue. If you are, I encourage you to begin to accept God's love for you today. It might be challenging at first but you can do it. Place your confidence in Him and you will begin to see a change in you. Love is patient, so be patient with yourself throughout the process. You are so worth it! Our King of Kings says so!

Written specifically for you,
Ms. Shandia Booker

Scriptures to Explore

For God is the King over of all the earth. Praise him with a psalm.
-Psalm 47:7 (NLT)

But you are not like that, for you are a chosen people. You are royal priests, a holy nation, God's very own possession. As a result, you can show others the goodness of God, for he called you out of the darkness into his wonderful light. -1 Peter 2:9 (NLT)

But the Holy Spirit produces this kind of fruit in our lives: love, joy, peace, patience, kindness, goodness, faithfulness, gentleness and self-control. There is no law against these things! -Galatians 5:22-23 (NLT)

Questions

Can you share a time when you struggled to accept God's love?

_____

_____

_____

_____

_____

_____

In what ways does your relationship with your father impact your relationship with God (positively or negatively)?

_____

_____

_____

_____

_____

_____

If you struggle to accept God's love, and you make a decision to accept God's love today, in what ways can that impact your life?

_____

_____

_____

_____

_____

_____

_____

_____

_____

Words of Encouragement

Girl, accept the fact that you are LOVED by the KING of all KINGS. Listen, in moments when I'm frustrated I remind myself that my dad is THE KING. He calls the shots and He has everything He needs to protect and provide for you. I'm sure you would have a sense of peace knowing that your father has everything he needs to take care of you. Now accept that your heavenly Father is the KING, He lacks nothing, He will provide for you and He will protect you. He will love you in a way that only a King can, and he will be as loving and gentle as possible in doing so. Girl, when you're older and start dating, always keep in mind who your Father is, and ask him to show you a young man who is after his own heart. #DaughterofTHEKING #RoyaltyinsidemyDNA #Princess #LovedbyaKING

Chapter 4

Glo on Girl

"When God said let there be light, He was giving you permission to shine."
- Marshawn Evans Daniels

Dear Brooklyn,

Dr. Martin Luther King once said "Darkness cannot drive out darkness, only light can do that". You are light! It is so important that you allow your light to shine. When you allow your light to shine by simply being yourself, your energy will radiate and lead other girls to let their light shine also.

The light that you carry has the potential to light a room and provide a sense of warmth. That's right, the light that you carry on the inside of you can bring warmth to a room full of people! Your "light" is your personality, your gifts, your talents, your smile, your laughter, and your character. There will be times in your life where you may feel pressured to minimize your shine, shrink down, or not allow the world to truly see your greatness. In those moments, you have to be brave enough to keep shining, trusting that God will keep you lit.

Girl, it's time for a *M.O.T (Moment of Transparency)*. There have been times in my life where I felt more comfortable blending in than I did standing out. Can you relate? I always had an understanding that success comes with critics. Because of this, I felt more comfortable containing my shine when I knew that my *light* was meant to radiate. This usually happened when I noticed that my light made others uncomfortable, causing them to say things such as, "Who does she think she is?" or "Girl, I heard her project wasn't really that good". You know some people highlight your weaknesses in hopes of dimming your light. They might not realize that by highlighting your weakness (with the intention to tear you down), shows their insecurities. The truth is, they may be struggling with understanding the gifts they carry. They may be going through a hard time in their own life or they may not be focused on cultivating the gifts that God gave them. That's why growing up you may have heard a loved one say, "Who are they?" Don't let "them" stop you from moving forward in your life.

Mathew 5:16 instructs us to "Let your light so shine before men, that they may see your good works, and glorify your Father which is in heaven." Letting our light shine brings glory to our Father in heaven. If, like me, you ever feel like diminishing your own light, remember that shining brings glory to our Father in heaven! We were meant to glow! God did not create you to be mediocre. He created greatness when He created you! Diminishing your light does not serve you well, and it's a disservice to those you are called to positively impact. The Bible says God's gifts are without repentance, so He won't take the gifts and greatness inside of you back. However, He wants the awesomeness inside of you to be seen. Diamonds shine, but did you know that they are made under pressure? They have to undergo a process before they hit jewelry store shelves. In that same way, we undergo a process and through our relationship with God and His love for us, He allows us to shine. Allow God's purpose within you to be your motivation to shine. Now glo' on girl and shine!!

Written specifically for you,
Ms. Shandia Booker

Scriptures to Explore

You are the light of the world-like a city on a hilltop that cannot be hidden. -Mathew 5:14 1(NLT)

No one lights a lamp and then puts it under a basket. Instead, a lamp is placed on a stand, where it gives light to everyone in the house. -Matthew 5:15 (NLT)

In the same way, let your good deeds shine out for all to see, so that everyone will praise your heavenly father. -Matthew 5:16 (NLT)

For God's gifts and his call can never be withdrawn. -Romans 11:29 (NLT)

Questions

Why is it important to let your light shine?

_____

_____

_____

_____

_____

_____

When another girl's light shines, does that mean you aren't "lit" anymore? Why or why not?

_____

_____

_____

_____

_____

_____

What barriers stand in the way of you allowing your light to shine? Explain below.

_____

_____

_____

_____

_____

_____

In what ways can you allow your light to shine at home, at school, and in your community?

_____

_____

_____

_____

_____

_____

_____

_____

Words of Encouragement

Glo on, with your Beautiful self! Girl, you better go for it! Work hard, allow others to see the gifts that God has blessed you with. Sing the song, play the sport, create the play, start the group, and write the book! Remember, being from the inner city does not take away from your light, in fact it adds to it. Listen, that GIFT you have, we all need. Don't sit on your gifts. Girl, share your gift with others. Be yourself and radiate your light in the space you are in. Don't allow anything or anyone to dim your light, and don't aim to dim the glow of others! #Letyourlightshine #GloOngirl #Jesuskeepsmelit

Chapter 5

Let Go, Forgive, & Live!

"It's one of the greatest gifts you can give yourself, to forgive. Forgive everybody."- **Maya Angelou**

Dear Brooklyn,

Girl, what I am going to challenge you to do takes courage! That's right, courage to make a hard decision even when you feel justified to make a different one. Most of us may not realize the importance of courage, however it is needed in order to let go, forgive and live! In your life you may experience hurt, offense, and others may upset you. When you experience these and other circumstances, it will be important for you to forgive others so that you can be at peace. Girl, forgiving someone is easier said than done because forgiving requires us to let go of resentment and retaliation. Forgiveness is one of God's most powerful tools that He has given us to move forward in life. Remember that forgiveness is for you and it's a PROCESS. It may not happen all at once, it just requires for you to take steps in the right direction. You deserve to give yourself what you need to proceed. Holding on to things we were never meant to hold onto is unhealthy and does not add value to our life. In fact, it can take our joy. Letting go, on the other hand, will help you! When you begin to let go of any offenses you are faced with, it will allow you to live a happier more fulfilled life.

Forgiving others becomes easier when you realize that most people do the best they have with the information they have at the time. I believe that people cannot give you what they don't have. For example, you can't expect someone to let you borrow $20.00 if they only have $10.00 in the bank. There are times when people hurt others intentionally, in those times remember that is not your fault. Sometimes it easy to harbor bitterness, or anger because someone did something to hurt us. Often times, how people treat you is a reflection of how they treat themselves. People can't love you correctly if they struggle to love themselves. It's hard for people to be kind to you if they're not kind to themselves.

When you harbor anger, or bitterness, your life can become more challenging. You may start seeing everything in your life from a place of hurt, rather than a place of hope. Anger is an emotion, that all of us have felt at some point. Expressing your anger is an important part of the forgiveness process, and a great starting place is between you and God. Talk to God about how you feel and keep it real with him. Girl, he can handle it. You can also seek wise counsel through a Counselor to help you process your emotions. You have to remember that the battle is not yours. The battle is His. He doesn't want His daughter walking around unnecessarily with anger and bitterness. He wants to take that off of you. He has your back and wants to make room for joy and for love to abound in you.

When people hurt us, God encourages us to forgive others as He forgives us. He forgives us regularly. While God tells us in His Word to forgive, He does not require us to become doormats. In an effort to avoid that, you can set boundaries. Setting boundaries can help you put forgiveness into action. For example, if a friend has an attitude, and as a result she disrespected you by speaking in a rude manner, you may want to have a conversation and communicate that when she talks to you that way, it makes you feel upset or even sad. Thus, moving forward, you may ask your friend to talk to you once she is calm and able to communicate respectfully. Boundaries can help improve relationships.

M.O.T (Moment of Transparency): Earlier I talked to you about the absence of my father and the impact that his absence had on my life. As I got older, his absence seemed to impact me more than what I realized. I talked to him about it and I shared my frustration. I'm sure he felt my anger, but I got to a point in which I chose to forgive him. Although our relationship is far from perfect, I no longer harbor bitterness towards him. I haven't yet figured out our relationship, but I am open to having one, with boundaries. The first step I had to take was forgiving him for not being there. I encourage you to extend forgiveness to those who have hurt you as well. Maybe you need to forgive your father, mother, a family member, acquaintance, or a friend for saying mean things about you and trying to damage your reputation. I challenge you to forgive them and our Father wants you to forgive them too. I would encourage you to communicate your concern, set boundaries, and FORGIVE.

Forgiveness is a process. You may be at a different point in the process than others. Remember that choosing not forgive, impacts how you live. Each step you take to let go and forgive is a step of courage. Holding on to bitterness, resentment and anger, impacts the way you live. You are not hurting the other person when you don't forgive. When you choose not to forgive, you only hurt and hinder yourself. Instead, choose to let go of the offense, forgive, and cast all your cares on God, allowing Him to handle the situation for you. This will enable you to live the life that you've been destined to live. God will gladly take your burdens and pain when you cast them on Him. He will provide healing and comfort to you when you need it. Lastly, forgiving others is an expression of love and we are called to love one another. God loves us enough to forgive us! That's something to be glad about. Isn't He wonderful?

Written specifically for you,
Ms. Shandia Booker

Scriptures to Explore

Instead, be kind to each other, tenderhearted, forgiving one another, just as God through Christ has forgiven you. -Ephesians 4:32 (NLT)

For if you forgive other people when they sin against you, your heavenly Father will also forgive you. -Matthew 6:14 (NLT)

Questions

Who do you need to forgive?

_____

_____

_____

_____

_____

_____

In what ways can forgiveness help you move forward in your life?

_____

_____

_____

_____

_____

_____

_____

_____

_____

What is stopping you from forgiving others?

_____

_____

_____

_____

_____

_____

Words of Encouragement

Girl, forgiveness helps lift the weight. We were not built to carry the weight of bitterness, anger, and rage. Our Father calls us to cast our cares on Him. He takes care of His children. Release the pain and the person who hurt or offended you. By releasing the offense, you will be liberated! When you forgive, you also allow God to heal you. If you need to set boundaries between you and another person, be sure to do so. Forgiveness does not give a person permission to treat you badly, it simply means you trust our Father enough to let him handle the people who have offended you. He's your protector, He will take care of you!! #LetgoletGod #Forgiveandlive

Validation is for Parking – Not IG, Facebook, Twitter

"Your worth and value is not based on how many people "like" you. You are worthy because He loves you."– **Shandia Booker**

Dear Brooklyn,

You are beautiful and wonderfully made! Remember, our Father chose you and set you apart. He created you for a purpose that only you can fulfill on this earth. He put detailed thought into you because you are His precious daughter. You are valuable. There's no doubt that God knew exactly what He was doing when he created you and even in all of your greatness, some people still may not like you. Guess what? That's okay! If someone does not like you, don't let that stop you from being great. Continue to let your light shine anyway, Glo on Girl!

MOT- Moment of Transparency: When I was your age, I thought that if I treated people nicely, and if I was a helpful person, that there would be no reason not to like me. Unfortunately, that is not always true. People choose not to like others for many different reasons, and honestly, they may struggle with liking themselves. You have to remember that people who may not like you are missing out on a friendship with one of the King's greatest creations, you! Girl, you have to remember not to live for the approval of others. People pleasing distracts you from walking confidently in your purpose.

Know that people don't set your value, GOD does! Your worth is not based upon their approval, validation, or celebration. You were worthy before any human decided to weigh in on your value. God sent his one and only son to die on the cross for you! That's how valuable you are to Him. You can't place value on that type of love.

As you navigate life and the world around you, you may find yourself seeking the validation of others. Growing up in the age of technology, you will have information at your fingertips which is amazing, but it can also trigger "approval addiction". A person may be struggling with approval addiction when their actions are dictated by the approval of others. Approval addiction is real, and if you are not careful you can put people in the place that God should be. Don't live to please people, live to please Him. Have you ever posted a flawless picture of yourself on social media? You know, that one pic where your hair is on point, your outfit is cute and the day you took the picture you had a good attitude (lol). You knew for sure your beauty was shining from the inside out? Then about 20 minutes later you only had 3 likes? You begin to wonder, "How?" You have 1000 friends. Only 3 likes? After another 20 minutes you only gained a few more likes. Finally, you made the decision to take your picture down. Girl, let me tell you, likes cannot and <u>should not</u> define who you are.

Sometimes when people don't think they are enough, they make decisions out of a place of insecurity to gain the approval of other people. If you find yourself making decisions solely based on what other people think, I encourage you to consider what may be making you feel insecure. Remember that you are ENOUGH and developing a good sense of self (understanding and knowing who you are, and what you're worth) is important. When people are comfortable in their own skin and embrace who they are, it is reflected in their decision making.

I'm going to ask you a few questions that I want you to answer honestly. Doing so will help you identify the root of your decision making.

Reflection

-Have you ever posted something on social media that you didn't really want to post, but you knew it would get a lot of likes?

-What happens when your Social Media "friends" don't like your post? Does that impact you negatively?

-Do you tear others down in hopes of building yourself up?

-Do you seek out validation from others consistently?

If you answered "yes" to any of the questions above, you might be making choices just to earn the approval of others. It's essential that you make choices from a place of self-confidence and confidence in God. It's not always easy, but the more you practice, the better you will become. Choices made out of a place of insecurity can often be disguised as the right choice, but they aren't typically the best choices. They may be based on an irrational belief such as "I am not enough, if I don't have approval from others". Self Esteem is the confidence and satisfaction in one's self, (as defined by Merriam-Webster). Having a healthy sense of self helps you to realize that nothing outside of you can make you or break you. NOTHING. If you want to start improving your self-esteem, I recommend giving yourself room to grow, surrounding yourself with people who are supportive, and identifying your strengths. My hope is that you begin to understand your worth and value and make the connection between being secure in who you are and making good decisions.

By reviewing the figure on the next page, you may become more aware of your decision-making mindset.

Written Specifically for you,
Shandia Booker

Figure 1. Insecurity versus Security

Insecurity	Security
Posting a meme that makes fun of people so your friends can like your status	Posting a funny meme that you can relate to and does not tear others down
Not wearing a shirt that you love because your friends hate the color	Wearing the shirt you love, regardless of what others think of it
Tearing another person down, because they are on the "glow up" and you are not where you want to be.	Complimenting or congratulating someone for reaching their intended goals. · Using their success as motivation to help you reach yours.
Posting a picture of yourself with your new shoes on, hoping to impress people	Posting of picture of yourself that serves as a good representation of who you are
Not applying to the college you want to attend because you are not confident that you will be accepted.	Putting your best forward and applying to the college of your choice. Keeping in mind that your value doesn't decrease or increase based on acceptance.
Attempting to block another person's blessing because you don't feel that they should glow brighter than you.	Praying for the success of others. You have a strong sense that if God can help them He can help you too!

Scriptures to Explore

Obviously, I am not trying to win the approval of people, but of God. If pleasing people were my goal, I would not be Christ's servant. -Galatians 1:10 (NLT)

And it is impossible to please God without faith. Anyone who wants to come to him must believe that God exists and that he rewards those who sincerely seek him. -Hebrews 11:6 (NLT)

What shall we say about such wonderful things as these? If God is for us, who can ever be against us? -Romans 8:31 (NLT)

Each time he said, "My grace is all you need. My power works best in weakness." So now I am glad to boast about my weaknesses, so that the power of Christ can work through me. -Corinthians 12:9 (NLT)

Words of Encouragement

I encourage you to build yourself up in Christ. Remember that you were valuable when you were a thought in the mind of our Father. Girl, don't build your self-esteem on the number of likes you get on social media, on your new outfit, or on your new hairstyle. That would be like building a house on sand, and we all know that a house that does not have a good foundation is quick to fall. Those things are like accessories, they may add to your look or your image, but they do not define who you are. Girl, remember whose you are. Place your faith in God and start to believe in yourself like never before! Before you post online ask yourself "Am I doing the most?" Am, I posting this in hopes of earning someone's stamp of approval? Girl, there's no greater validation than the love of God. Remember that you are validated by The King. #ValidatedbytheKing #Christlikesme #Worthsaving #Kingdomapproved

Chapter 7

The Glo Up is REAL

"If you can't figure out your purpose, figure out your passion. For your passion will lead you right into your purpose."
- Bishop *T.D. Jakes*

Dear Brooklyn,

The Glo up is real! As you begin to grow up, you will discover so much about who God created you to be! He has a specific purpose for your life! When your passion meets your purpose, you will impact the world positively. According to Merriam-Webster passion can be defined as a strong liking, desire for, or devotion to some activity, object, or concept. Purpose can be defined as the reason for which something exists or is done, made, or used. God gives us all gifts according to his will. Girl, when you begin to uncover your purpose you will have such a sense of joy!

At your age, it is likely that you are discovering who you are and what you love. Your life will be full of stages of exploration of purpose. 1 Corinthians 12:4-11 (MSG) teaches us that each person is given something to do that shows you who God is. According to the scripture "The variety is wonderful" and includes wise counsel, clear understanding, simple trust and much more! Often times, when you carry out your purpose you will utilize the gifts our Father has given you.

Begin to align your gifts with your interest. If you are struggling with identifying things that interest you, start with prayer and ask Him to reveal those things to you. Following prayer, I suggest taking an interest inventory. There are many online such as the Career Clusters or Strong Interest Inventory. After you obtain the results, find volunteer opportunities that will allow you to work in the areas that were highlighted for you.

Faith without works is dead, so please keep in mind that your purpose will require work! When you are passionate about the work you do, your passion will fuel your ability to bring your project to completion. When you begin to walk in your purpose, you will have increased opportunities to share your gift with others. It is imperative that you plan and prepare for whatever it is that you are purposed to do. For example, if you want to become a teacher, you can research how much schooling it takes, what type of degree you need, and you can also interview people in the field. You can also review lesson plans. Even at your age now, you can practice teaching by teaching your friends, asking to lead a class at Sunday school, or tutor students in school. When you are in alignment with the purpose God has for your life, you develop focus and discipline.

While discovering your purpose, you may admire someone else's gifts as well. Celebrating someone else and their gifts can encourage that person to continue to press forward. Everyone can use encouragement; just be careful not to envy the gifts that others carry. Our gifts should work together to advance the Kingdom.

There are instances, in which you may find yourself so focused on another individual's purpose that you lose sight of your own. Check in with yourself and remember the importance of staying in your lane. Sometimes people take their eyes off of what God has called them to do, and they focus on or criticize another person. By focusing on another person's lane, you can become easily distracted from what God has called you to do. There is room for everyone. There is no need to compete when it comes to living out your purpose. No one can operate in your lane the way that you can.

God has purposed me to provide encouragement, resources, and guidance through my work as a School Counselor and in other areas of my life. I believe NBA coaches provide their teams with encouragement, resources, and guidance as well. However, I am not going to become a coach for the NBA. Why? That is not the lane in which my gifts will manifest. I enjoy sports, but I don't have the talent to coach a NBA team. I understand that my lane requires too much of me to stay focused on someone else's. When you remain focused on your gifts and purpose, you will find success in your lane.

Once you begin to walk in your lane, the Father's light will shine through you. You will notice a shift within you and a glow that can't be denied. Your purpose, passion, preparing, and provision will be tied into His plan for you. Discover God's purpose for your life! While you may experience challenges and "glowing pains", don't give up on your purpose, pray and push through. God equips you for the challenges that you will face. Glo up girl, you got this because He's got you!

Written specifically for you,
Ms. Shandia Booker

Scriptures to Explore

*"For I know the plans I have for you" says the Lord. "They are plans for good and not for disaster, to give you a future and a hope." -*Jeremiah 29:11(NLT)

*The thief's purpose is to steal and kill and destroy. My purpose is to give them a rich and satisfying life. -*John 10:10 (NLT)

*For God's gifts and his call can never be withdrawn. -*Romans 11:29 (NLT)

*For we are God's masterpiece. He has created us anew in Christ Jesus, so we can do the good things he planned for us long ago. -*Ephesians 2:10 (NLT)

Each person is given something to do that shows who God is: Everyone gets in on it, everyone benefits. All kinds of things are handed out by the Spirit, and to all kinds of people! The variety is wonderful: wise counsel, clear understanding, simple trust, healing the sick, miraculous acts, proclamation, distinguishing between spirits, tongues, interpretation of tongues. -1 Corinthians 12:4-11 (MSG)

Questions

List your gifts and talents below. Think about what you do well and what makes you unique. Remember, qualities such as leadership, organization, humor, generosity, etc. are gifts. Share yours below.

_____

_____

_____

_____

_____

_____

Identify hobbies and interests that you can spend time researching about. Do you believe the hobbies and gifts you have are related to your purpose?

_____

_____

_____

_____

_____

_____

_____

_____

_____

Are there times when you feel disqualified or afraid to walk in your purpose? If so, share strategies that can help you move past your feelings.

_____

_____

_____

_____

_____

_____

What step(s) can you take today that will help you fully walk in your purpose?

_____

_____

_____

_____

_____

_____

Words of Encouragement

Girl, you've been created on Purpose for a Purpose. Your gifts will not drain you, they will fuel you. When you operate in your gift, you will impact others positively. The Father's purpose for you is bigger than what you can even imagine. You have to trust that He will provide the provision (money, connections, resources, school, etc.) that you may need to birth your purpose. God will use you in a mighty way when you remained focused on Him. When I say the Glo up is real, it is! Just as you grow from a child to an adult, your purpose will grow with you. It is your job to plan and prepare. You don't have to know everything now, you just have to be committed to remaining a student of your craft. God will open doors and provide new opportunities for you to shine. Glowing up is a process and it's worth it! Why? Because you are worth it! #Glowupgirl #Liveonpurpose #Growtoglo

Chapter 8

Laugh Out Loud (LOL)

"A cheerful heart is good medicine, but a broken spirit saps a person's strength" -**Proverbs 17:22 (NLT)**

Dear Brooklyn,

Enjoy your life! Life is full of ups and downs, and that's why you have to spend time laughing. Girl, did you know that laughter is medicine for your soul? It is ok to enjoy life, be silly, and humorous. Appreciate the moments that provide you the opportunity to Laugh out Loud. Laughter is contagious!

It is so important that you find joy in the small things in life. We were not meant to carry around a heavy load. I believe you can lighten your load by letting go and allowing God to fill your heart with *warmth* and joy and laughter. The type of laughter that fills the room with pure joy! I definitely have a goofy side. I can be really silly! I think my closest friends see that side of me the most. I love to break out in song, and please believe me when I tell you that my gift IS NOT singing. I mean, it's hard for me to catch the right tone, LOL. Singing allows me to express myself in a joyful way, and it gives me a chance to laugh at myself.

With so many responsibilities, I have to remind myself to laugh at myself. Like moments when I trip up the steps, or times in which I'm singing along to a song I've known forever and just realized that the lyrics I thought I knew aren't the actual lyrics. I'm usually convinced that the lyrics I've come to know and love are the actual lyrics, until I meet up with friends who know the real words and suddenly, I realize that I had the lyrics all wrong. I laugh at myself in those instances. I mean, who trips while going up the steps, and confuses song lyrics (LOL)? I do!

Research suggest that laughter can sooth tension, help relieve stress and provide a sense of relaxation. As I researched the effects that laughter had on humans, one thing remained constant; laughter (in isolation) may not be responsible for all of the positive effects but spending times with loved ones and enjoying life collectively impacts our lives positively.

When challenges or difficult times come, we often forget that the joy of the Lord is our strength. We have to press into God during these times and remember that He is a very present help. I encourage you not to allow those times to rob you of your smile, your laughter, and your joy. Have you ever encountered someone that helped to brighten up your day by sharing their gift of the ability to make you laugh? I mean they made you laugh so hard, that you forgot that your day wasn't going as planned. Those moments are a reminder of the sweet presence of God. They remind us to stop, breathe, smile, and laugh. I believe that is why He connects us to people. They remind us of his presence even during times of challenges.

If you are having a difficult time, you may find yourself wanting to disconnect from other people. During those times I encourage you to stay connected to our Father. I encourage you not to isolate yourself totally. First spend some time with God in prayer. Ask Him to send you understanding friends, who can help bring a smile back to your face. Pray for healthy relationships that will provide spaces in which you can laugh and enjoy your life. Remember in those spaces, you don't have to aim to tear anyone down by laughing at them, but use laughter as a tool, to build one another up.

It is really important to develop a sense of balance in life. Incorporating laughter into your life is essential for your well-being! Girl, take some time to do something that will allow you to have fun. Don't allow life to pass you by without cherishing moments of laughter. Remember that God gives us the gift of laughter. His word reminds us in Proverbs 17:22 that "a cheerful heart is good medicine". Find some time to laugh out loud today!

Written specifically for you,
Ms. Shandia Booker

Scriptures to Explore

We were filled with laughter, and we sang for joy. And the other nations said, "What amazing things the LORD has done for them. -Psalms 126:2 (NLT)

He will once again fill your mouth with laughter and your lips with shouts of joy. -Job 8:21 (NLT)

She is clothed with strength and dignity, and she laughs without fear of the future of the future. When she speaks, her words are wise, and she gives instructions with kindness. -Proverbs 31:25-26 (NLT)

A cheerful heart is good medicine, but a broken spirit saps a person's strength. -Proverbs 17:22 (NLT)

A glad heart makes a happy face; a broken heart crushes the spirit. -Proverbs 15:13 (NLT)

Enjoy prosperity while you can, but when hard times strike, realize that both come from God. Remember that nothing is certain in this life. -Ecclesiastes 7:14 (NLT)

So I concluded there is nothing better than to be happy and enjoy ourselves as long as we can. And people should eat and drink and enjoy the fruits of their labor, for these are gifts from God. -Ecclesiastes 3:12-13 (NLT)

Words of Encouragement

Girl, call up your closest friends and have a girls' day! Do something relaxing and fun, and just be yourself! Sing in the rain, make silly video clips using different apps, or have a karaoke contest. Bring cheer to one another. Laughter can improve your mood and the mood of those who around you. Take some time just to laugh! When is the last time you decided to do that? You know our Father has the best sense of humor, share in his gift. #LOL #Soulmedicine #Cheerfulheart

Chapter 9

Joy, Pain, & Peace

"Give me that joy I can't explain. Add extra peace that'll ease my pain.
I want that love that'll never change. Give me that, give me that"
— **Kirk Franklin & Mali Music**

Dear Brooklyn,

Joy and Pain is like sunshine and rain. As I write this letter, that song continues to come to mind. I know you're thinking "What song?" The song I'm referring to is called "Joy & Pain" by Frankie Beverly and Maze. Girl, if you haven't heard of that group, ask your mom or grandmother about them! (Lol). This letter is all about joy!

There is a difference between joy and happiness. Happiness can be a fleeting emotion, joy is a state of being. The joy that God gives resonates deep within your soul, the joy our Father gives us is amazing. The Bible says the "The joy of the Lord is your strength" (Nehemiah 8:10). I've heard many people say that you can't appreciate the sunshine if you haven't experienced rain. Other people have suggested that one may struggle to appreciate joy if they haven't experienced pain. I believe joy resonates on a deeper level than happiness can reach.

No matter what may be going on in our lives, when we learn to trust God and accept the peace that He provides, He can fill our hearts with joy. I have learned to press into it! Naturally, I want to figure things out, see other people happy, and have a sense of happiness myself, but sometimes life circumstances impact my desire to be happy. When I think about who God is, how he loves me and what he's done, joy abounds in my spirit. I may feel frustrated, but God reminds me that all things will work out for my good.

Another way I can describe joy to you is the state of being in alignment. When I am aligned with my divine assignment and I am walking in my purpose, I am overwhelmed with joy! The good news is, joy is available for you too! I believe, that God gives us joy that helps to strengthen us to continue to do what he calls us to do.

As Christians, we are not exempt from facing pain and being frustrated. The Bible tells us in James 1:2-3 to "consider it pure joy" when we face trials of any kind because our faith is being tested. When our faith is tested we have the opportunity to strengthen our faith and our perseverance. When you rejoice in the Lord, He will give you joy that is indescribable. I encourage you to press past your feelings and press into joy today!

Scriptures to Explore

Consider it pure joy, my brothers and sisters, whenever you face trials of many kinds, because you know that the testing of your faith produces perseverance -James 1:2-3 (NIV)

May the God of hope fill you with all joy and peace as you trust in him, so that you may overflow with hope by the power of the Holy Spirit. -Romans 15:13 (NIV)

But the fruit of the Spirit is love, joy, peace, forbearance, kindness, goodness, faithfulness, gentleness and self-control. Against such things there is no law. -Galatians 5:22-23 (NIV)

Questions

Why do you think God encourages us to "consider it pure joy" when we face trials?

_____

_____

_____

_____

_____

_____

_____

_____

_____

_____

When you are having a rough day, what can you do to remember to accept the peace that God gives?

_____

_____

_____

_____

_____

_____

Explain a time that you experienced the joy that God gives. How was that experience for you?

_____

_____

_____

_____

_____

_____

_____

_____

_____

_____

_____

_____

_____

Words of Encouragement

Girl, go play "Give me that" from Mali Music and Kirk Franklin. After you listen to the song, reflect on what it is like to experience the joy that God gives! Try your best to trust God with your challenges. It won't be easy, but it will be worth it. Give yourself the chance to acknowledge how you feel. If you feel hurt, tell God directly how you feel. He will comfort you during those times in your life. If you are going through a particularly challenging time in your life, you may find therapy to be helpful. There are Christian Counselors that can help you navigate difficult times, make good decisions, and process pain. I believe seeking the help you may need is an expression of the love you have for yourself. Allow love to lead, and by doing so, you will feel a sense of God's love, peace, and joy! The joy that He gives you, girl the world can't take it away. #JoythatIcantexplain #Peace2easethepain #PressintoJoy

Chapter 10

Your Reaction, Your Response, Your Responsibility

"Don't be a hard rock, when you really are a gem"
– **Lauryn Hill**

Dear Brooklyn,

Girl, life can have its challenges and choosing to respond instead of choosing to react requires patience and presence. You will encounter people who may trigger you, press your buttons, or try to annoy you. The truth is we all do, and you may also trigger someone else. I encourage you to remember that your reaction and your response is your responsibility! This can be a challenging lesson to learn. You will encounter many different people in your life and you may enjoy some encounters more than others. You might encounter someone who gives you a hard time or those who do not treat you with the respect you deserve.

You are not responsible for another person's behavior and another person is not responsible for yours. When people project their negative feelings and emotions onto you, you can choose to <u>respond</u> instead of <u>react</u>. That's right, I said you can <u>choose</u>. When you feel that someone is being rude or disrespectful, pause, take a deep breath, and think before you speak.

I know that growing up in the inner city produces a fight in you. I grew up in the inner city too, so I know the importance of standing up for yourself. I also understand the "fight" you experience when you feel that someone has disrespected you. God will use the "fight" in you for greatness. I remember being frustrated one day and asking God "If I let go, who will protect me?" God replied, "Let go and I'll protect you". In that moment, His response gave me a sense of relief. Growing up as a black girl in the inner city, you learn how to become strong and self-sufficient. You learn how to figure things out, not to give up easily, and work with what you have. I believe it produces grit in you that sets you apart. Being resourceful and working with what you have is a skill, so I encourage you to continue to build that skill as you develop new ones. Develop the skill of letting go and relying on God, especially when you're faced with a situation that is pushing you to react. You are not alone, and when it seems like your back is against the wall, God is there protecting you and making a way.

Girl, just remember that the battle isn't yours, it belongs to the Lord. You don't have to figure everything out on your own in your own strength. Trust Him with your battles, He will always have your back, and He will never leave you, even when it seems that your "opponent" has won. It may appear that your opponent is seemingly successful at blocking your blessings, or embarrassing you in front of others, telling you off, or treating you in such a way that made you feel small. Remember that is not really winning and they have nothing on you. Winning does not require tearing others down.

In times like these, reserve your energy for assignments that matter. Girl, choose not to engage in every verbal battle that comes your way. Use your energy wisely by relying on the God inside you. By doing so, you will not fail or lose. Many times, our natural inclination is to react to others. You know, someone gets "smart" with you, so you want to react by getting smart back. Girl, here is a W.O.W. (word of wisdom) don't jump too quickly and give your power to someone else who is struggling to convey their feelings in a respectful manner or respect you. When you feel stirred, I encourage you to take a moment, pause, think before you speak and set a boundary. Girl, this is a lesson to stick in your back pocket. Even as an adult, I have to encourage myself to do the same thing.

MOT-Moment of Transparency: girl this can be difficult. We have all reacted instead of responding at some point in our lives. Responding requires patience with yourself and others. Everything and everyone does not deserve your reaction. For example, I've been on the phone with customer service representatives who may have had a difficult day before talking to me. I may have had a difficult day as well. Their tone may come across less than ideal and I have to remind myself to slow down and pause. When I am able to do that, my response helps the conversation to go smoother. In the same way, when we choose to react, situations can become more difficult than we want them to be.

In these moments, PRAY. Ask God for discernment and ask him to give you the words to say. Also, remember the importance of listening. You have to learn to listen not only with your eyes (what their body language saying to you), and your ears, but also listen with your heart. If someone is speaking to you in a way that may be belittling or disrespectful (and it's not their pattern or typical behavior), you may want to respond by saying, "It sounds, like you are having a rough day, can I pray for you?" When you listen with your heart, you can truly hear what the person is saying even if it wasn't communicated well. Ask God to help you be patient, slow to speak, and slow to anger.

As I mentioned, in Chapter 5, it is important to set BOUNDARIES with people. When I was younger, I didn't feel totally comfortable with expressing my boundaries. I was more concerned with how the other person would feel if I expressed my boundary. As I grew, my voice did also. Boundaries help show other people what you will and will not accept. Choosing to respond instead of react is not a "punk" move. It actually takes self-control and it shows that you are mature. You will feel empowered by the decision you've made not to give away your power.

Responding is a skill you will build over time. When you are developing a skill, it is important for you to be patient with yourself. We become better at learning new skills through practice. If you are triggered this week, practice choosing to respond instead of react. If you react, don't come down hard on yourself; simply ask God to help you work on your ability to respond to people instead of reacting. You may need to ask someone to give you a few minutes, take a walk, or express to them that you need more time to get back to them. Give yourself what you need, so that you don't react. This will produce a better response. Girl, I'm working on this with you, so you are not alone. I'm sure other readers are as well. I encourage you to **practice the skill** of responding by reading the following scenario.

Scenario

A situation that has occurred between two girls named Chanel and Laniah. Chanel was having a rough day at school because she failed her math test. Laniah, who earned a B on the test, asked Chanel if she needed any help studying. Chanel yelled, "Why would I get you to help me? You're not special, who needs your help anyway?"

Laniah may be tempted to get smart with Chanel. If she were to *react* instead of *respond* she may say something like:

"I know you aren't getting smart with me, with your mean self. Keep talking to me like that, and you'll see. That's why your failing!"

If Laniah choses to *respond*, she may say:

"When you speak to me that way, I feel disrespected. When you can talk to me in a calm way we can re-visit this conversation".

As you can see. you can choose to *respond* by clearly communicating your boundaries, and not further stirring the situation. When you are faced with a situation like this, choose to expend your energy wisely. Laniah has a choice to make, she can allow Chanel's attitude to impact her attitude, or she can choose to respond instead of reacting. This simple tool will help you, as you deal with others. God gives us peace, power, and a sound mind. Don't give your power to your emotions, choose to *respond* instead of *react*.

Written specifically for you,
Ms. Shandia Booker

Scriptures to Explore

When she speaks, her words are wise, and she gives instructions with kindness. -Proverbs 31:26 (NLT)

Be kind and compassionate to one another, forgiving each other, just as in Christ God forgave you. -Ephesians 4:32 (NLT)

A gentle answer deflects anger, but harsh words make tempers flare. -Proverbs 15:1 (NLT)

People with understanding control their anger; a hot temper shows great foolishness. -Proverbs 14:29 (NLT)

Questions

Write about a time in which you could have responded instead of reacted.

_____

_____

_____

_____

_____

_____

_____

_____

_____

When faced with a challenge, what can you do to remind yourself to stop and think before you speak?

_____

_____

_____

_____

_____

Identify boundaries that you can set that will be helpful when dealing with conflict.

_____

_____

_____

_____

_____

_____

_____

_____

_____

_____

_____

_____

_____

_____

_____

_____

Words of Encouragement

Girl, God will work with you on this, just as he works with us all. Be encouraged, knowing that God will give you the peace you need to respond instead of react. He will also give you words to communicate your boundaries in a clear manner. Remember, choosing to respond does not make you a punk! It shows that you are unwilling to give your power away and that you trust God to take care of you and the situation. Let go of handling everything on your own and allow God to handle things for you. #Choosingtorespond #Godisforme

Chapter 11

Loving the Skin You're In!

"Freedom is being who you are, unapologetically"
- **Dr. Robyn Smith**

Dear Brooklyn,

Girl, it's so important that you begin to embrace the skin you are in! When God created the human race, He created so many different shades, hues, and colors. From light skin to dark skin, beauty can be found all around you.

As an African American woman, I understand the complexity of messages that we receive about who we are and what is considered beautiful. I have seen girls struggle with feeling like their beautiful brown skin is too dark, while others struggle with feeling like their skin was not dark enough. In America, our battles with skin hue can be traced back to slavery. While standards of beauty are often sent through television and magazines, you have to remember that you don't have to subscribe to them. It's okay to embrace your skin, even if it looks different than those who are around you.

As I've shared with you throughout this book, God created you exactly how you should be. Whether you have a darker skin complexion or a lighter skin complexion, He chose your color with His purpose in mind. Chocolate, Cinnamon, Brown Sugar, Vanilla, and Carmel too, your skin is beautiful, and so are you. Having a lighter complexion or a darker complexion doesn't make you inferior or better than anyone else. Here's what you have to remember and take hold of: He thought you were to die for, you are the apple of His eye, girl remember that you are of the HIGHEST kind and quality. Your Father is the KING of all kings. Your color is a reflection of Him. Your job is to take care of the skin that He has given you, embrace it, and recognize the beauty in it. Girl, loving yourself is an inside job. Once you begin to believe what God says about you, the confidence that you will carry as a result of embracing who you are will radiate from within.

The truth is everyone has melanin in their skin. Some people have more than others, and that depends on a number of factors, including genetics. By embracing the skin you are in and walking with confidence, you will set a new beauty standard. You will help another person do the same. When conversation about skin color occurs, often times conversation about hair textures follows. Embracing who God called you to be doesn't mean other people will validate you. For example, if you prefer to have your hair in braids but your friends prefer to have their hair silk pressed, you have to be comfortable and confident in your decision to rock the style that you prefer. Girl, embrace who you are! I encourage you not to pull another girl down for rocking their style differently than you. Whether you rock natural hair, braids, sew-ins, or twists you have to do what works for you. The goal is to maintain healthy hair. Your preferences and journey will likely be different than someone else's and that's okay!

I encourage you to look in a mirror and write down some things that you love about yourself! If you are struggling to see the beauty of your complexion, talk to God. I would also encourage you to Google positive women who look like you and as you recognize the beauty in them, remember that beauty exist in you.

There are two documentaries that delve further into colorism. They are titled Dark Girls & Light Girls. These documentaries explore the hurt that many African American girls feel as a result of people saying hurtful things about their skin color. I encourage you to view the documentaries with an adult who can help you process how you feel. The documentaries will also help you to understand the experiences and the perspective of other girls.

The journey to loving yourself can feel like a challenging process, but it's worth it. The moment you embrace who you are, you will feel empowered to do what God calls you to do. Yes, you may look different than someone else, you may do things differently as well, but that is the BEAUTY of it all. Be who He called you to be, whether you have someone who approves of you or not. Girl, you're beautiful, love yourself!

Scriptures to Explore

To acquire wisdom is to love oneself; people who cherish understanding will prosper. -Proverbs 19:8 (NLT)

As the Father has loved me, so have I loved you. Abide in my love. -John 15:9 (NIV)

Then God said, "Let us make human beings in our image, to be like us. -Genesis 1:26 (NLT)

Questions

Share a time that you've struggled to love the skin you are in. What factors caused you to struggle with loving your skin?

_____

_____

_____

_____

_____

_____

_____

_____

_____

_____

Identify ways that media messages have influenced your own personal beliefs about beauty.

_____

_____

_____

_____

_____

_____

_____

_____

_____

_____

_____

Identify 3 positive attributes and characteristics about yourself that you consider beautiful.

_____

_____

_____

_____

_____

_____

_____

_____

_____

_____

Words of Encouragement

Girl, sometimes the world sends messages that can make you feel as though you aren't enough. The truth is, you're more than enough. You have to accept that God loves you and accept who He has called you to be. In doing so, you will not feel like you are more inferior than someone else, and you won't carry yourself as though you're superior. Instead, you will begin to notice growth and more self-confidence in your own life. The melanin in your skin was given to you on purpose. I believe that you have greatness in you, and our KING is going to use all of who you are for His will to manifest in your life. #Melaninprincess #lovetheskinyourin #Beautiful #GlorytoGod

Chapter 12

Write Your Vision, Align Your Mission

"Think like a Queen. A Queen is not afraid to fail. Failure is another stepping stone to greatness." - **Oprah Winfrey**

Dear Brooklyn,

This chapter is for you to reflect on what you have read and plan to apply the knowledge to your life. God is inside you, you will not fail! Don't allow fear to get in the way of you going after your dreams! This chapter is designed to help you reflect and think about creating a life you love! Writing your vision helps you accomplish your mission. By answering the questions and beginning to plan your next steps, you will have the opportunity to gain clarity and start planning your goals for the future. Writing can be a healthy way to express your thoughts and feelings, get personal, be clear, have fun, and ask questions if you need assistance. Glo on girl!

Gems of Wisdom

Start by reflecting on what you've read so far, what resonated with you? What gems have you gained from reading chapters 1-11? Write down the biggest lesson you've learned. #IssaGem #Gemcollection #WOWMoments

_____

_____

_____

_____

_____

_____

_____

_____

_____

_____

_____

_____

_____

_____

_____

_____

_____

_____

_____

Affirmations Fit for A Princess

Affirmations; Encouragement (You are worth it!) Encourage yourself below. What are qualities that you love about yourself? What have you embraced about yourself? What makes you BEAUTIFUL?

_____

_____

_____

_____

_____

_____

_____

_____

_____

_____

_____

_____

_____

_____

_____

_____

_____

_____

_____

_____

_____

_____

_____

What Will I Forgive in Order to Live?

Use this space to identify things you can afford to let go. Are you holding on to anger, forgiveness, or bitterness? Share your feelings and begin the process of letting go. Remember when we choose to throw things away, we don't usually go in the trash to pick them back up. What are you going to release?

_____

_____

_____

_____

_____

_____

_____

_____

_____

_____

_____

_____

_____

_____

_____

_____

_____

_____

_____

My Passion & His Purpose

Your vision, should align with his PURPOSE for your life. Begin to pray and ask God what his purpose is for you.

Think about some things you are passionate about. What fuels you? What drives you to achieve your dreams? Write about those things below:

_____

_____

_____

_____

_____

_____

_____

_____

_____

_____

_____

Based on what you've written above, if you were able to help someone else, how would you incorporate your passion in doing so?

_____

_____

_____

_____

_____

_____

_____

_____

_____

_____

_____

My Vision

Next, write a Vision Statement. Vision is usually a big picture idea. Close your eyes and imagine who you want to become. Where do you envision yourself in the future? This can include character qualities as well as ideas related to your purpose.

_____

_____

_____

_____

_____

_____

_____

_____

_____

_____

_____

My Mission

Lastly write a **Mission Statement**. What are you currently pursing to achieve your vision? What steps are you currently taking or what steps do you need to take today to become the person you envision?

_____

_____

_____

_____

_____

_____

_____

_____

_____

_____

_____

_____

_____

_____

_____

_____

_____

_____

_____

_____

My Action Plan

Use this space to create an action plan on how you will incorporate what you've read into your life. I have given you space to create 3 goals, and a place to list the steps you'll need to take to accomplish your goals. Be specific and give yourself a timeframe. You will find that writing out your plans, helps you achieve your goals. I encourage you to return to this section of the book to record the outcome of each goal so you can see your progress!

Here's an example:
Goal: My goal is to get accepted into a college that has a great Computer Science program by the Fall of 2021.

Follow Up Steps: I will research and visit schools that have Computer Science programs. I will complete my college application. I will submit my application by December 2020. I will choose a University by May 30, 2021.

Outcome: I was accepted into 3 schools. I chose to go to the University of Pittsburgh and major in Computer Science. I will start school in the Fall of 2021.

Goal #1:

_____

_____

_____

_____

Follow Up Steps:

_____

_____

_____

_____

Outcome:

_____

_____

_____

_____

Goal #2:

_____

_____

_____

_____

Follow Up Steps:

_____

_____

_____

_____

Outcome:

_____

_____

_____
_____

Goal #3:
_____
_____
_____
_____

Follow Up Steps:
_____
_____
_____
_____

Outcome:
_____
_____
_____
_____

Remember that according to Proverbs 16:9 we make our plans, but the Lord will establish our steps. How encouraging is it to know that God will establish our steps? Even when the steps look different than you may think, find solace in the fact that God, our Father, is establishing (setting or fixing) things on your behalf. When you reach a goal, share it out and encourage someone else. #Ontheglowup #DearBrooklynLoveYourself.

Scriptures to Explore

Then the Lord answered me and said: "Write the vision and make it plain on tablets, that he may run who reads it. -Habakkuk 2:2 (NKJV)

We can make our plans but the Lord determines our steps. -Proverbs 16:9 (NLT)

For I know the plans I have for you," declares the LORD, "plans to prosper you and not to harm you, plans to give you hope and a future. -Jerimiah 29:11 (NIV)

Commit your actions to the LORD, and your plans will succeed. -Proverbs 16:1 (NLT)

God is within her, she will not fall; God will help her at break of day. -Psalm 46:5 (NIV)

Now all glory to God, who is able, through his mighty power at work within us, to accomplish infinitely more than we might ask or think. -Ephesians 3:20 (NLT)

For as he thinketh in his heart, so is he. -Proverbs 23:7 (KJV)

For God is working in you, giving you the desire and the power to do what pleases him. -Philippians 2:13 (NLT)

Conclusion

Girl, I hope that after reflecting on what you've read in this book you were able to pick up some gems to help you navigate life. Remember life has it's up and downs, but God is a very present help! In the words of Whitney Houston "sometimes you'll laugh, sometimes you'll cry, life never tells us the when's or whys, but when you've got friends to wish you well, there comes a point when you'll exhale!" You have a friend in Jesus, and if God is for you, who can be against you? The Bible says for every season, there is a time (Ecclesiastes 3:1). Time can be one of your most valuable resources (it's one thing in life you can't get more of). Use your time to pursue your passion, develop your gift, grow in loving relationships, help others, laugh out love, and talk to God! Work hard, have faith, and trust Gods timing! Remember that if "something" is meant for you, he will ensure that you receive it. Align your mission with your vision and continue to "glo" into who God has called you to be. #Valued #Dreamsfrommyking #PurposedfortheGloup

Notes

Chapter 1
Salters, J.N. "35 Maya Angelou Quotes That Changed My Life." The Huffington Post, TheHuffingtonPost.com, 7 Dec. 2017, www.huffingtonpost.com/jn-salters/35-maya-angelou-quotes-th_b_5412166.html.

Chapter 2
Pine, Joslyn T. Wit and Wisdom of America's First Ladies: a Book of Quotations. Dover Publications, 2014. (E-Copy)

Chapter 3
"How He Loves [Radio Version] [Version] Lyrics." Lyrics.com. STANDS4 LLC, 2018. Web. 30 May 2018. <https://www.lyrics.com/lyric/29416859>.

Chapter 4
Esq, Marshawn Daniels. "When God Said, 'Let There Be Light," He Was Giving YOU Permission to Shine! #Godfidence Pic.twitter.com/CIW2AbKFMF." Twitter, Twitter, 29 Mar. 2015, twitter.com/marshawnevans/status/582321560234524672?lang=en.

Chapter 5
Johnson, Zach. "Maya Angelou's 15 Best Quotes." E! Online, E! News, 28 May 2014, www.eonline.com/news/546030/maya-angelou-s-15-best-quotes-regarding-love-forgiveness-humility-and-survival.

Chapter 7
Jakes, T.D. "If You Can't Figure out Your Purpose, Figure out Your Passion. For Your Passion Will Lead You Right into Your Purpose. #WednesdayWisdom." Twitter, Twitter, 18 Jan. 2017, twitter.com/bishopjakes/status/821688845972414464?lang=en.

Chapter 9
"Give Me Lyrics." Lyrics.com. STANDS4 LLC, 2018. Web. 30 May 2018. <https://www.lyrics.com/lyric/32345125>.

Notes

Chapter 10
"Doo Wop Lyrics." Lyrics.com. STANDS4 LLC, 2018. Web. 30 May 2018. <https://www.lyrics.com/lyric/15953171>.

Chapter 11
"Soul Food: 12 Helpings from Dr. Robin Smith." Oprah.com, www.oprah.com/own-super-soul-sunday/food-for-thought-12-bytes-from-dr-robin-smith/all.

Chapter 12
Co, Emily. "8 Valuable Life Lessons From Oprah Winfrey." Business Insider, Business Insider, 3 Nov. 2014, www.businessinsider.com/oprah-winfrey-quotes-life-lessons-2014-11.

Acknowledgments

God- Thank you for being my King of Kings and loving me the way that you do. I'm thankful for your vision for my life. I'm thankful for your warm and loving spirit.

To my Mom, Annette Parker- Hey Beautiful! I am so thankful for you, you were my first model of love strength. I've watched you persevere through life. Your beauty and strength inspire me. I pray that God continues to bless you. I'm grateful that God chose you to Mother me and I'm hopeful that the love you give others will return to you. I love you so much, I pray God blesses you EXPONENTIALLY!

To my Stepdad, Wayne Hopewell- Thank you for working hard every day to provide for my mom and our family. I'm truly thankful for your support over the years. Thank you for all you've done and continue to do.

To my Father, George C. Booker- Thank you for your words of kindness and support. I pray that our relationship will continue to evolve. I pray that God continues to keep his hand on you. May God bless you richly!

To My Grandfather, Cleveland Parker- Grandad you were blind, but you never loss your Vision. Thank you for teaching me (in your own way) to have vision. You were always on a mission and you lived your life to the fullest. I miss you immensely. I love you and I pray that you are resting peacefully in the arms of our Father.

George Booker - Thank you for being my BIG brother. You taught me more than you know. Thank you for your silliness, and encouragement. I'm grateful that God has given me a brother like you. Thank you for expanding our family and making me an Auntie of future leaders. *Shout out to Don,* I believe God will continue to develop you and you will positively impact the world.

Dewayne Hopewell- Thank you for being YOU! Your work ethic and caring heart will take you far in your life. Thank you for keeping me current, and helping me with technology. I'm so grateful that God gave me a little brother as AWESOME as you.

Teresa R. Hunt- Thank you for partnering with me on my purpose project. Your professionalism, and love for publishing is evident in the services that you provide. Thank you for being an amazing editor and motivator throughout this process. I appreciate you!

Michelle Mitchell- Thank you for writing the *Foreword* and believing in my vision. I believe that God is going to do exceedingly abundantly more than you can ask or think. Your hard work and dedication is inspiring and I appreciate your help during this process.

Acknowledgments

Special thanks to my Amazing Aunts

Thank you for being the fabulous women that you are. Thank you for encouraging me to persevere. Thank you for prayers, encouragement and direction. Thank you for love, laughter and light. I LOVE YOU!!

Special thanks to All of my Wonderful Friends

Thank you for your friendship and encouragement. Your support, kind words, & encouraging messages mean so much to me. Thank you for your strength, and for simply being who you are in my life. I believe that GOD is going to do AMAZING things in your life. I'm thankful for each and every one of you. I believe that my life is richer because you are in it, and you serve as a reminder of God's goodness.

Special thanks to Shavonda, Jenifer, Lydia, Michelle, Barbara & Syl

Special thanks to my Sunday School Teachers, Professors, School Counselors, & Those who inspire me

Thank you for coming in to my life and helping me grow. I pray that you continue to inspire people to pursue their dreams!

Special thanks to Pittsburgh Temple Corps-Salvation Army-

Reaching communities and teaching the love of Christ

Special thanks to Mount Ararat Baptist Church-

Where the message of God has been shared with love

Special thanks to Readers

Thank you for allowing me to see the details of God working in my life. Thank you for choosing to read this book, I pray that God will enrich your life. I'm grateful for your support!

About the Author

Shandia Booker, MSEd, is a certified School Counselor in the state of Pennsylvania. Having grown up in the inner city of Pittsburgh, PA, Shandia is passionate about helping the next generation of Queens succeed and reach their goals. She understands the importance and need for girls to know and embrace their value amidst their circumstances. Shandia has clinical experience working with underprivileged and marginalized populations. With a goal to empower pre-teen girls as they transition from elementary to middle school, Shandia developed a program titled Love Yourself that has impacted hundreds of girls in the City of Pittsburgh. Shandia received the Region 4, 2017 Regional Homeless Advocate of the Year award by the Pennsylvania Department of Education. Shandia enjoys writing, spending time with friends & family, and creating programs that celebrate and empower girls to pursue their purpose in life. You can learn more about Shandia at: www.ValidatedByTheKing.com